SPIDERS
BIGGEST! LITTLEST!

by **Sandra Markle**

Photographs by Dr. Simon Pollard

Boyds Mills Press

Garden Orb Web Spider

Some spiders are big.
Some spiders are little.

See the little spider near the big spider's mouth?

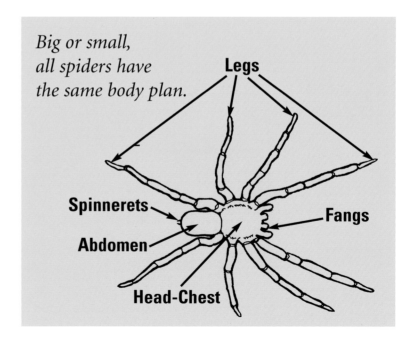

*Big or small,
all spiders have
the same body plan.*

Legs

Spinnerets

Fangs

Abdomen

Head-Chest

Some spiders also have big parts—
like this Brown Jumping Spider's eyes.

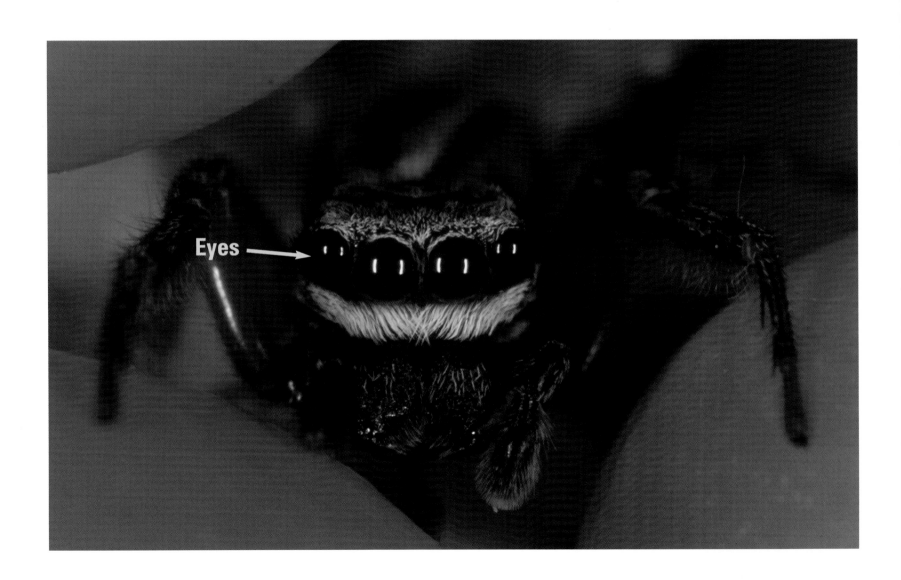

How does it help a spider
to be big or little?

How does it help some spiders
to have extra-big parts?

To find out, you'll need to see
how a spider lives.

**Cave Sheet
Web Spider**

First, all spiders are hunters.
They must catch other animals, or *prey*,
to eat.

That's why this Cave Sheet Web Spider is
about to attack an insect.

Not sure which one is the spider?
Start counting.
All spiders have eight legs.
Insects have only six.

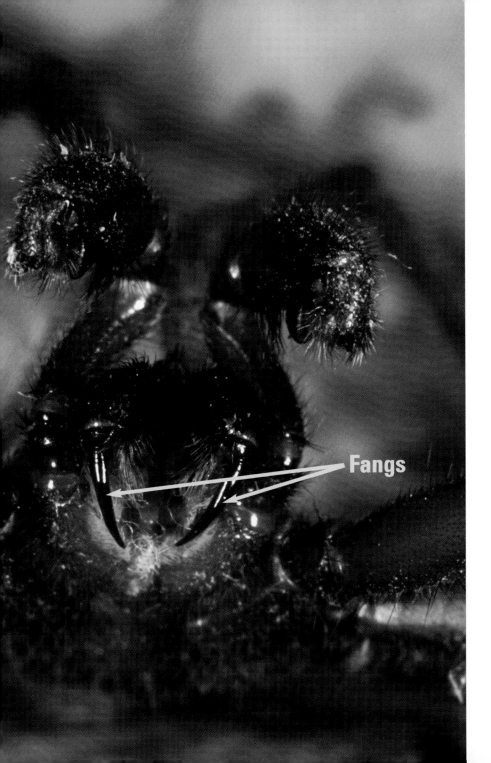

Fangs

So a spider's body is built to help it be a good hunter.

For one thing, all spiders have weapons to help them kill their prey—fangs.

Even little spiders have fangs.

**Peruvian Pink-Toe
Tarantula**

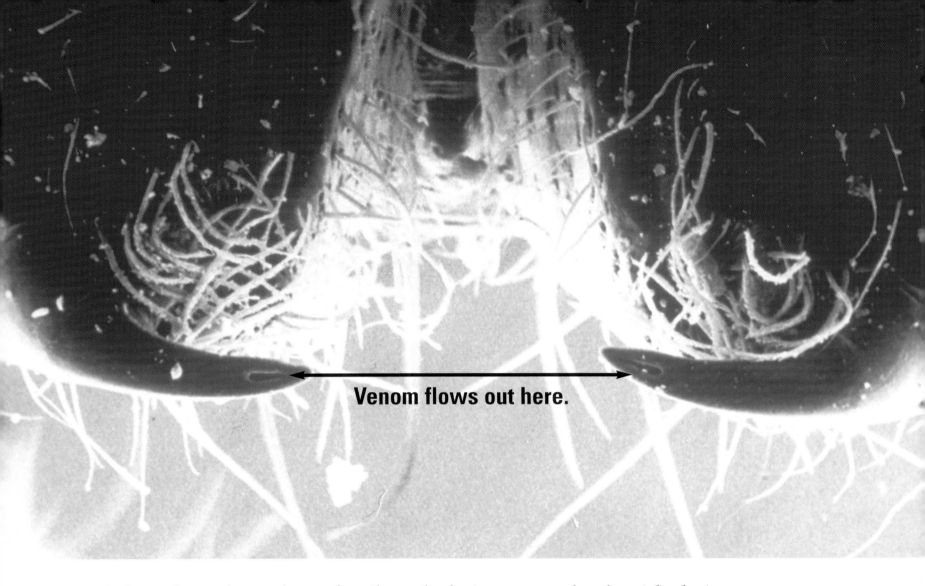

Venom flows out here.

And though spiders of one family stab their prey to death with their fangs, most kill another way.

Take a close look at this spider's fangs. When the spider bites, poison called *venom* (VEN-um) flows out of the fangs.

The Ground Hunting Spider has really big fangs.

These extra-big fangs help it catch prey that other spiders would not risk attacking.

That's because it can inject venom without getting too close to prey that could fight back, such as beetles.

This is a Goliath Bird Eater Spider.

It's just big all over. In fact, it's the world's biggest kind of spider.

With its legs spread out, it may be as big as a dinner plate.

How does it help the spider to be big?

The Goliath Bird Eater Spider can catch prey that are too big for most spiders to hunt.

Sometimes it really does eat small birds!

The food it eats helps the Goliath spider grow bigger.

But a spider's soft body parts are inside a stiff body suit.

So when the spider grows, its old body suit splits open.

Then the slightly bigger spider crawls out, wearing a new body suit that quickly hardens.

For some spiders, being little is the key to success.

This Crab Spider is so little it can hide inside a flower.

That's how this sneaky hunter was able to surprise the bee.

After grabbing the bee by the neck, the Crab Spider used its fangs to inject venom and make the kill.

Some spiders, like this jumping spider, hunt by chasing down prey.

Having extra-big eyes helps the jumping spider grab insects that are too quick for other spiders to catch.

**Sri Lankan
Jumping Spider**

As soon as the mosquito landed, the jumping spider spotted it.

And the spider used its big eyes to judge just where to pounce.

GOTCHA!

Furry Jumping Spider

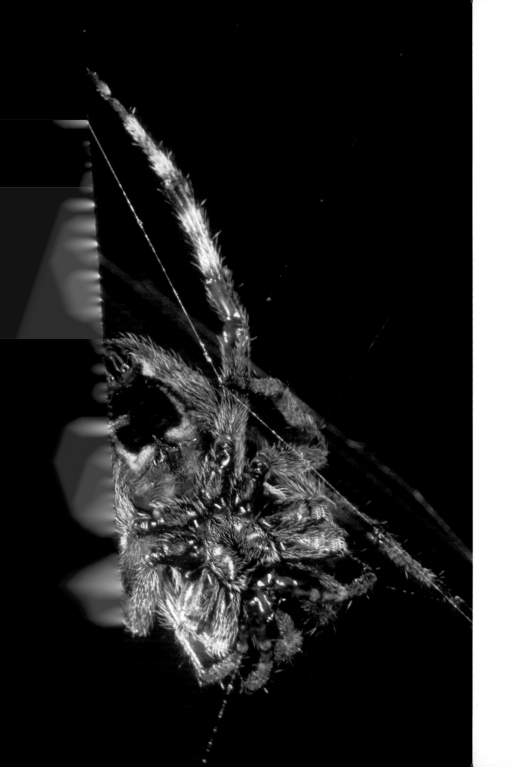

It is night.

The Garden Orb Web Spider is pulling a long thread out of its rear end.

This thread is called silk.

Another thing all spiders do is make silk.

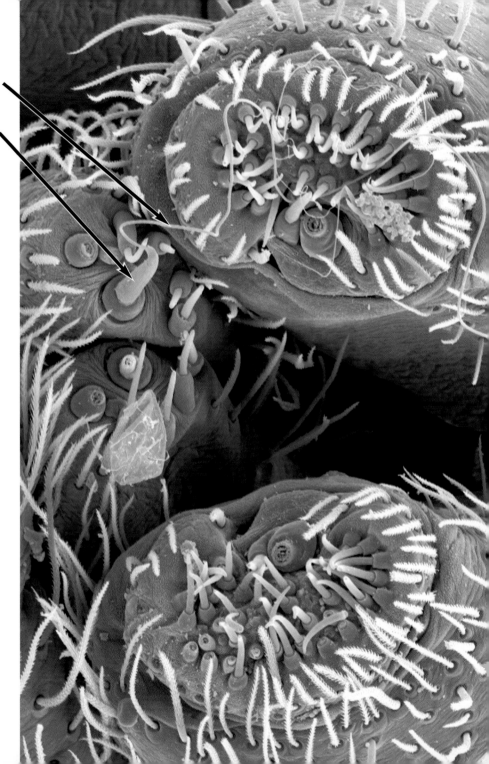

Silk

Spigot

These are a spider's spinnerets—
the part where the silk oozes out of
hose-like spigots.
The spider pulls the silk into strong
threads.

Spider silk has many uses.
A lot of spiders use silk as a safety line.
A silk thread can stop a spider from
falling from high places.
Silk has another good use, though.
The Garden Orb Web Spider is making
something to help it hunt.

Can you guess what that is?

It's a silk web.

This trap makes it easy for the spider to catch flying prey.

Once an insect is caught in the trap, the Garden Orb Web Spider bites it to inject venom.

Then the spider wraps its prey in more silk.

That way the prey can't escape while the venom does its job.

This big spider (on the left) is a female Golden Orb Web Spider.
About the size of a man's hand, this kind of spider
builds the world's biggest web.
Its silk trap may be as wide as two cars parked side by side.

How could such a big web help the spider?

Female Golden Orb Web Spiders make their living by catching flying insects that are too big for other spiders to trap.

Here, the spiders seem to be floating in air because you can't see their webs.
Being hard to see makes the webs an even better trap.
Unlike most spiders, Golden Orb Web Spiders also hook their webs together.
That makes super traps as much as two stories tall!

Golden Orb Web Spider silk is so strong the spider's web can last for years. Local fishermen even used to take the spider's web to use as a fishing net.

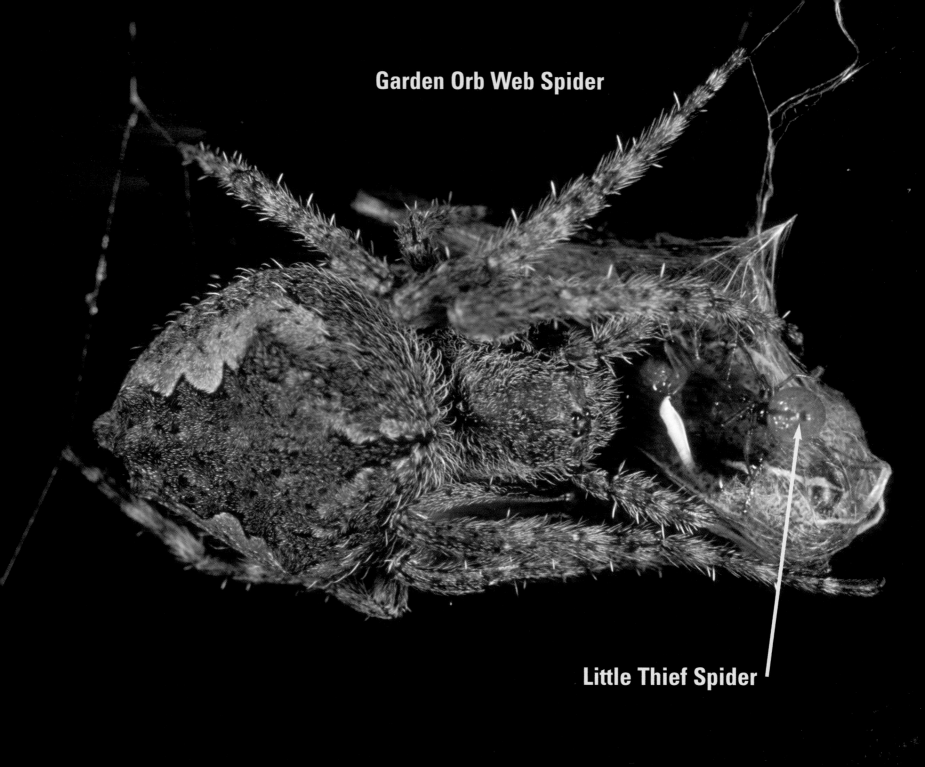

Garden Orb Web Spider

Little Thief Spider

Remember this little spider?

As tiny as the tiniest raindrop,
the Little Thief Spider is one of the
world's littlest spiders.

Can you guess how being so little
helps it?

Like the Crab Spider, the Little Thief
Spider is small enough to be sneaky.

All spiders have little mouths.
So to eat, the Garden Orb Web Spider
threw up juice from its stomach onto
its prey.

This turned the prey's soft parts into
soup.

As the big spider sucks in its food,
the Little Thief Spider slips up and
steals some of the big spider's meal.

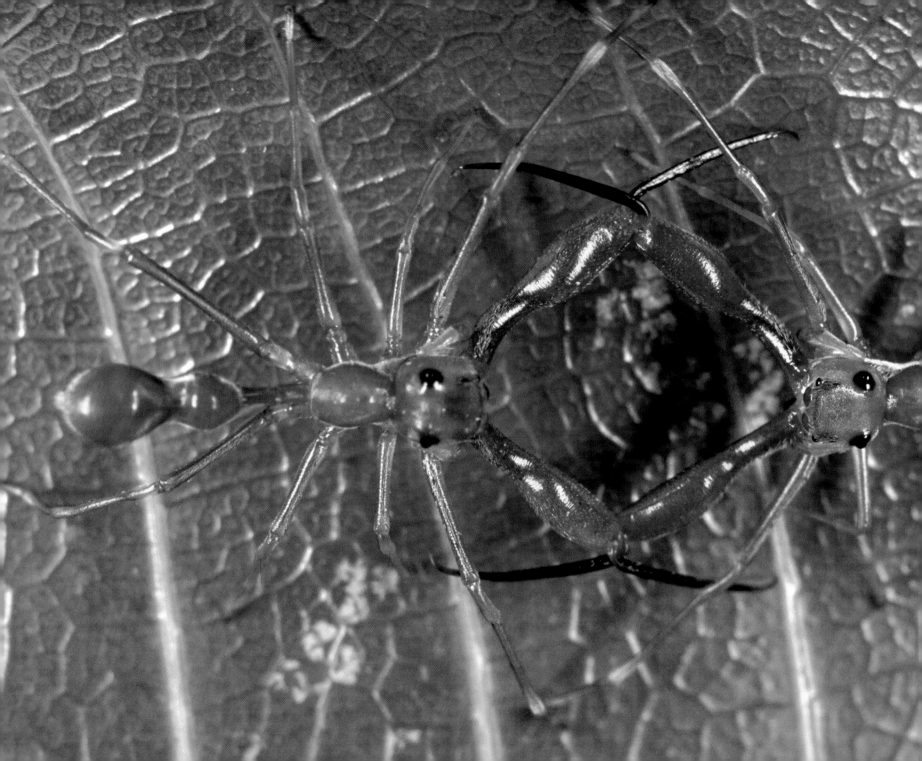

You've seen how having extra-big parts can help some spiders make a living.

But the male Ant-Mimic Spider has super-big fangs for another reason.

The males clash their fangs together like swords to duel for a nearby female.

Something else all spiders do is mate and have babies.

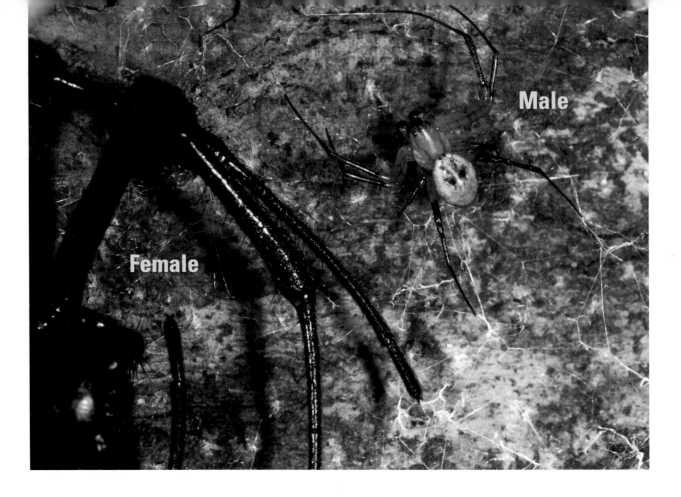

Take another look at the female Golden Orb Web Spider.
The little spider next to her is a male—her mate.
Most female spiders are bigger than the males.
A female Golden Orb Web Spider can be as much as four hundred times bigger.

But why does a female spider need to be bigger than the male?

Female spiders have to make eggs.

So the female's body needs to be big enough to do that job.

And females need to be able to catch bigger prey than males.

Producing eggs takes extra food energy.

Did you see that the eggs were wrapped in a silk case?
Female spiders use their silk to protect their eggs.

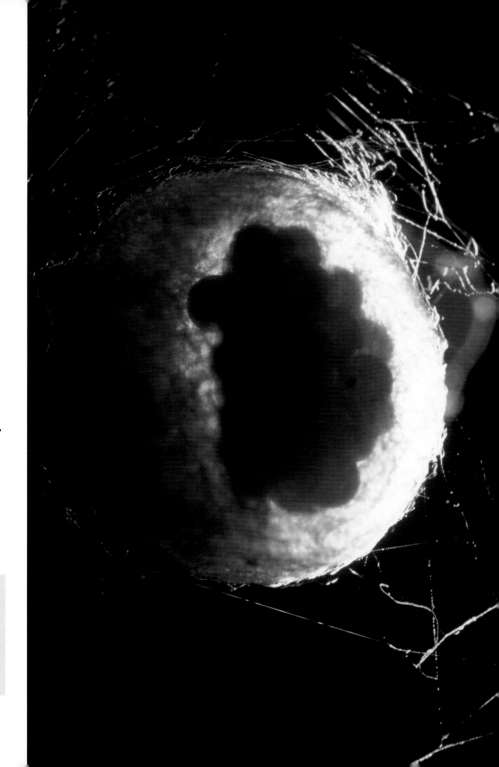

Look at all of the baby spiders inside this web!
The Nursery Web Spider watches over her babies.
For a baby spider, growing up is all about becoming as big or as
little as it was meant to be.
A spider's size is its very life.
Being big or being little—or even having extra-big parts—is how
each different kind of spider has adapted to
being a success in its own special part of the world.

Where in the world do these spiders live?

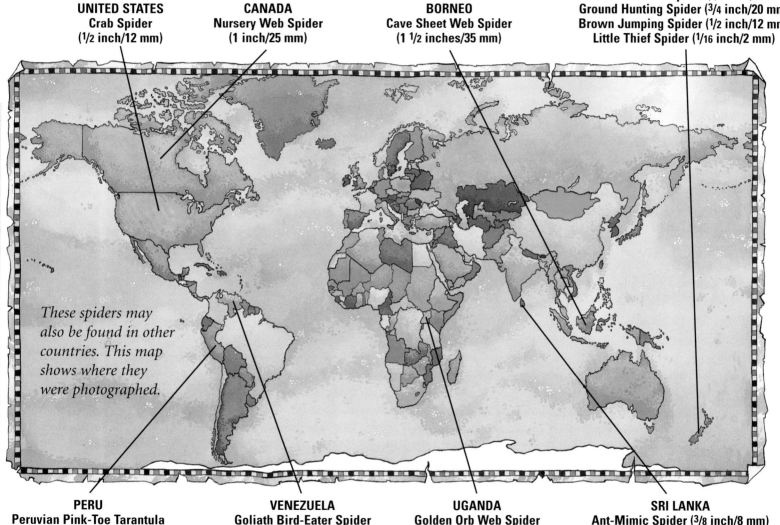

NEW ZEALAND
Furry Jumping Spider (1/2 inch/12 mm)
Garden Orb Web Spider (1/2 inch/12 mm)
Ground Hunting Spider (3/4 inch/20 mm)
Brown Jumping Spider (1/2 inch/12 mm)
Little Thief Spider (1/16 inch/2 mm)

UNITED STATES
Crab Spider
(1/2 inch/12 mm)

CANADA
Nursery Web Spider
(1 inch/25 mm)

BORNEO
Cave Sheet Web Spider
(1 1/2 inches/35 mm)

These spiders may also be found in other countries. This map shows where they were photographed.

PERU
Peruvian Pink-Toe Tarantula
(2 1/2 inches/98 mm)

VENEZUELA
Goliath Bird-Eater Spider
(4 inches/100 mm)

UGANDA
Golden Orb Web Spider
(male: 1/4 inch/5 mm;
female: 1 1/4 inches/30 mm)

SRI LANKA
Ant-Mimic Spider (3/8 inch/8 mm)
Sri Lankan Jumping Spider
(3/8 inch/8 mm)

Spider Words You Learned

Fang: A knife-like part used to stab prey.
Prey: An animal the spider catches to eat.
Silk: A special fiber the spider makes and uses.
Venom: Liquid poison that flows out of the fangs.
Web: A silk trap some spiders build.

Surprising Facts About Spiders

*Spiders have taste buds on leg-like parts near their mouth. They can taste what they touch.

*If a young spider loses a leg, it can regrow it.

*Spider silk is the strongest natural fiber in the world.

*Most spiders can go a month without eating. Some big tarantulas can go a year.

Published by Boyds Mills Press, Inc.
A Highlights Company
815 Church Street
Honesdale, Pennsylvania 18431
Printed in China

First edition, 2004
The text of this book is set in 18-point Minion.
Visit our Web site at www.boydsmillspress.com

10 9 8 7 6 5 4 3 2 1

With love for Elijah Beckdahl as he grows up
—S. M.
To Millie, my wonderful daughter
—S. P.

Acknowledgment: The author would also like to thank Dr. Simon Pollard for sharing his expertise and enthusiasm. And a special thank-you to Skip Jeffery for his help and support.

Photo Credits: All photos by Dr. Simon Pollard

Note to Parents and Teachers: The books in the BIGGEST! LITTLEST! series encourage children to explore their world. Young readers are encouraged to wonder. Then they are guided to investigate how each animal depends on its special body features to be successful in its particular environment.

"Each plant or animal has different structures that serve different functions in growth, survival, and reproduction. An organism's patterns of behavior are related to the nature of that organism's environment, the availability of food, and the physical characteristics of the environment." National Science Education Standards as identified by the National Academy of Sciences.

Front cover: Goliath Bird Eater Spider (left) male Golden Orb Web Spider (right)
Back cover: Crab Spider

Library of Congress Cataloging-in-Publication Data

Markle, Sandra.
  Spiders : biggest! littlest! / by Sandra Markle ; photographs by Simon Pollard.— 1st ed.
  p.   cm.
  ISBN 1-59078-190-2 (alk. paper)
  1. Spiders—Juvenile literature. [1. Spiders.] I. Pollard, Simon, ill. II. Title.

QL458.4.M35 2004
595.4'4—dc22

2003026794